A Life Deserves Nine Cats

A Life Deserves Nine Cats

Poems　　　**Drawings**
Ron Heard　**Sue Schindler**

A Life Deserves Nine Cats
ISBN 978 1 76109 642 6
Copyright © text Ron Heard 2023
Copyright © illustrations Sue Schindler 2023

First published 2023 by
Ginninderra Press
PO Box 3461 Port Adelaide 5015
www.ginninderrapress.com.au

Sue: to…Jess, Ruth and Ailsa,
who have always encouraged me to draw!

Ron: to…Moon-Cat, wild and beautiful

Sue says, 'I graduated from the Queensland College of Art many years ago. It was only after a cat came into my life that I began to draw again. She provides an endless variety of beautiful poses, and I now draw her every day.'

Ron says, 'I never had a cat while growing up, but the first things I got when living independently were a fridge, a kitchen table and a cat.'

1 ceiling cat

a small window under the eaves
gave light to the roof space
and a view
high over Brisbane and the river

when we first climbed there
we found an old sheet
from the Courier Mail
two photos –

the Story Bridge
illuminated for the Royal Visit

Marilyn Monroe
entertaining the troops in Korea

a thing to keep
as part of the house archives
we said

but the cat
loved perhaps the warm bird smell
perhaps the crisp fragile feel at the base of her claws
as she shredded it

2 dream cat

cat   nineteen years old
sleeps most of the time
finds her way into my dreams

she is in the library

striding through the reserve collection
curling up on a keyboard
demanding food in the lunchroom

I say
>see how she weaves between my legs
>she is my cat

the librarian says
>but you call her
>Kitty Shcherbatskaya
>she belongs to Russian Literature

I say
>no one really owns a cat

weakening the arguments on both sides

the librarian says
>OK
>we'll let you have her
>on extended loan

3 three-legged cat

after the accident
the crushed leg
and the amputation
we kept the cat indoors
for two weeks
when we let him out
he went to the above-ground pool
jumped onto its inch-wide rim
and walked
with water on his left
a six-foot drop on his right
stepped carefully over some branches
under others
turned
(a hesitant three legged turn)
walked back
came inside
demanded a lap
and slept

4 city cat

a small shop
on the edge of the CBD
the edge of the gardens
just enough space for essentials
paper   envelopes   staples
coffee   sugar   tim-tams
sandwiches   crisp salads
and a whole wall
of cat food

I had not realised
how many other workplaces
have a secret cat

5 sporadic cats

                neighbours' cat in my lap
                purring acupuncturist

tortoiseshell cat in the moonlight
shimmering all colours
        and none

                distant thunder
                      at my side
                      the cat purrs

    three a.m.
    cat wakes me
    purr or growl?

                cat on my lap
                faces left
                purrs in time with my heart

6 instinctive cat

I open all the windows
most birds fly towards light
this one's instinct is to fly higher
twice each lap
she thuds the ceiling

dodges the towel
as I try to catch her
and flies faster loops

the cat watches
sings a note mixed with purr and growl
as if he could croon the bird
into his paws

the bird settles on a ledge
blue-grey wings   rufous body
perhaps a wood swallow

hoping she will quieten
I spend the evening in the dark

at first light she flies through a window
into the dawn breeze

the cat raids a drawer
finds a thick pair of socks
spends an hour in mock killing

7 cat of many changes

I dig through shallow soil   then rock –
Brisbane polymetamorphics
that quickly split at the mattock's blow
and remember the time   after garden work
a stray cat sat beside me
and shyly licked sweat from my back

swinging the mattock   I repeat her names –
Anna Magdalena   I called her   as part of a sequence
Anna after one of the finest women I know
sometimes Anna Pest or Anna Mirabilis
and when she greeted me nose to nose   Anna Kissed

cold rain falls
but I'm glad
to have this task to do for her

I split more rock

she brought my life a random tortoiseshell grace
I accepted her restless nights
she accepted the times I went away
we shared quiet hours   friendship   warmth
until age and cancer brought her
slow fading then quick death

I lay her   wrapped in my finest towel
among the polymetamorphics

8 big cat & 9 little cat

her ginger cat got old and failing
he waves in the wind   she said
until he took his last cat choice
and found a secret   private place
to die

she grieved

in time she said
a life deserves nine cats
and went to seek another in the line

came home with two

both ginger

I bought the kitten for me   the cat for himself   she said

she loved the silliness of the kitten –
playing tigers   hiding   being close
admired the strength and gravity
of the male with golden eyes

slowly the male taught the kitten
skills for life
and the kitten taught the older one
how to be skittery again

0 unseen cat

we learn to draw a cat
assembling a list of parts
ears   face   whiskers
body and tail
each part a familiar set of lines

hard to unlearn
see what's there
and draw
edges
shadows
places where there's a
break of curvature
hollows
texture

but this isn't right either –
you get a porcelain cat
as though flesh
reaches to the tips of the fur

you have to draw
what the eye doesn't see
muscle and ligament beneath the skin
liquidity
shoulder bones
dreams of movement

then you make

a cat
that can walk through long grass
without disturbing a stalk

a cat that is also a shadow

a cat half a second before the pounce

www.ingramcontent.com/pod-product-compliance
Lightning Source LLC
Chambersburg PA
CBHW071039080526
44587CB00015B/2687